CONTENTS

INTRODUCTION

The week of Passover should be a joy for everyone; at the Seder service, unlike other Festivals, the food forms an essential part of the celebration. However, Passover is sometimes seen as a problem - a notoriously expensive and exhausting time. The first night is often the culmination of days of cleaning and shopping and the second night marks the beginning of a week of strenuous cooking and eating - followed by fatigue.

The PASSOVER MENU PLANNER is designed to take the worry out of cooking and provide dozens of ideas for fresh and healthy food. There is a strong emphasis on vegetarian and lighter dishes and all the recipes are marked with the description MEAT, MILK, PAREV or VEGETARIAN. There is also colour-coding to help you choose the type of meal you want.

PINK - is for the MICROWAVE. This is not fast food. It is adventurous cooking using the microwave to speed up some of the stages.

GREEN - is for HEALTH-CONSCIOUS dishes, many completely vegetarian, some with fish and meat, but all with less fat and sugar than normally associated with Passover.

BLUE - is for recipes which can be prepared in advance or are simply TIME-SAVING. This does not mean expensive packaged items. With careful planning and cooking ahead or by choosing simple, fresh ingredients a delicious meal can be trouble-free.

There are no recipes for chicken soup, knaidlach or plava. For these - and many other traditional foods - everyone has their favourite method. The Seder meal, too, is probably a combination of well-tried and successful dishes. The menu planner has been devised to bring some added sparkle to the familiar Pesach food, leaving you and your guests feeling lighter and happier.

A NOTE ON INGREDIENTS

The recipes call for mainly fresh ingredients, including fish, meat, poultry, fruit and vegetables. Although the Sephardim are permitted to eat Kitniot (peas, beans etc) these have been omitted. Of course all packaged food should be supervised and marked 'Kosher for Passover'. Certain products mentioned (e.g. olive oil, fresh cream) may not be available in all areas. In this case, an alternative should be selected.

QUANTITIES

The recipes are designed to serve four people, as part of a three-course meal. However, if you want to provide more generous quantities or are entertaining a crowd, increase the quantities (and the cooking time for microwave recipes), or choose several different dishes for each course.

STARTERS

LEEKS WITH RED PEPPER RINGS

Parev. Vegetarian

7OO g/1 1/2 lb small leeks
3 - 4 tbsp chicken or vegetable stock
1 - 2 tsp olive oil
225 g/8 oz red peppers, de-seeded and cut into rings
salt, black pepper.

To serve : vinaigrette

1. Wash the leeks very well, making sure there is no grit inside. (Split larger ones horizontally as it makes them easier to clean). Trim into even lengths and drain well.
2. Put the leeks in a dish with the stock, cover and cook on HIGH for 5-6 minutes. Leave to stand for 1-2 minutes; they should be tender but not too soft. Drain and keep the stock for another use.
3. Heat the oil in a dish on HIGH for about 30 seconds, add the pepper rings and toss to coat with the oil. Cook for 2 minutes until they are slightly wilted but still a little crisp. Season and leave to cool.
4. Arrange the leeks in a circle with the peppers in the centre. Sprinkle over a little vinaigrette and serve the rest separately. This salad is best cool, but not chilled.

POTATO BALL SOUP

Milk. Vegetarian

700 g/1 1/2 lbs large potatoes
225 g/8 oz carrots
1 bunch spring onions
few cauliflower florets or celery sticks
75 ml/3 fl oz boiling water
salt, pepper
450 ml/3/4 pt vegetable stock
15 g/1/2 oz butter
300 ml/1/2 pt milk

1. Using a melon/potato baller cut out balls from the potatoes and drop them, with the remaining part of the potatoes, into cold water. Cut the carrots into fine sticks. Finely chop the spring onions and roughly chop the cauliflower or celery.
2. Put the potato balls in a bowl with the boiling water and cook on HIGH for 4 minutes, or until just tender. Drain and season well.
3. Put the rest of the potatoes with the cauliflower or celery and half the carrot sticks in a dish with 150 ml/1/4 pt vegetable stock and cook on HIGH for 5 minutes. When the vegetables are soft, put them in a blender with the rest of the stock and blend until they are smooth.
4. In a separate bowl, heat the butter on HIGH for 40 seconds, add the chopped onions and the rest of the carrot sticks and cook for 3 minutes.
5. Mix these with the cooked potato balls, pour over the soup puree and stir in the milk. Reheat the soup gently, taste for seasoning and serve hot.

Note: You can keep this soup warm on a low setting.

AUBERGINE WEDGES

Parev. Vegetarian

450 g/1 lb aubergines
2 large onions, chopped
2 tbsp olive oil
1/2 tsp sugar
1 tsp lemon juice
salt, pepper
1 egg, beaten

For the garnish: 4 tbsp thick mayonnaise, sliced radishes, sliced gherkins, stuffed olives or red pepper cubes

1 Prick the aubergines and cook on HIGH for 5 minutes or until soft. Leave to cool slightly, remove the seeds and scoop out the flesh.
2 Saute the onions in the oil in a frying pan over high heat until brown. Put in a blender or food processor with the aubergine flesh, sugar, lemon juice and seasoning, and process until the mixture is smooth. Stir in the egg.
3 Place an upturned cup in the centre of a shallow 9 inch round dish. Pour the mixture round the cup, smoothing it out to make it quite flat. Cook on MEDIUM for about 7-8 minutes, or until the aubergine mxiture is just coming away from the edges. Leave to cool and cut into wedges.
4 Spoon over the mayonnaise, covering the surface completely, and garnish with thin slices of radish, gherkin or olive, or cubes or diamonds of red pepper.

CELERIAC SOUP

Milk. Vegetarian

1/2 lemon
1 celeriac (about 500 g/1 lb 2oz)
1 tbsp oil
1 onion, finely chopped
450 ml/3/4 pt light vegetable stock
salt, black pepper
300 ml/1/2 pt milk
2.5 cm/1 inch piece ginger root, peeled

1 Squeeze the lemon juice into a bowl of cold water. Peel the celeriac with a vegetable parer, removing any brown parts. Chop the celeriac into fairly small pieces, discard the spongy centre core, and immediately drop the pieces into the acidulated water.
2 In a bowl heat the oil on HIGH for 1 minute, add the chopped onion and cook for 2-3 minutes, or until soft.
3 Drain the celeriac and put in a dish with 150 ml/1/4pt of the stock, cover and cook on HIGH for 7 minutes.
4 Puree the celeriac with the onion and the rest of the stock in a blender and season with salt and pepper.
5 Put the milk into a jug. Grate in the ginger root and heat on HIGH for 1 minute. Pour the milk into the blender with the celeriac puree. Blend again until the mixture is smooth, taste for seasoning and add a little more vegetable stock or milk if the soup is too thick.

SPINACH AND PATE PARCELS FOR CHICKEN SOUP

Meat

275 g/10 oz chicken livers
1 tbsp oil
1 onion, finely chopped
600 ml/1 pt chicken soup
salt, pepper
450 g/1 lb fresh spinach

1 First make the chicken liver pate. Preheat the conventional grill. Wash the livers and remove any grisly bits. Pat them dry with absorbent kitchen paper, then grill on a rack for about 4 minutes on one side. Turn them over and continue for a further minute.
2 Heat the oil in a small frying pan, add the onion and cook over high heat until the onion starts to brown, then pour in 1 tablespoon of chicken soup.
3 In a blender or food processor, process the chicken livers with the onion. Season well and add another tablespoon of soup if the mixture is very stiff. (You should be able to spoon it out but it should not be too liquid). Leave the pate to cool.
4 Cut off the spinach stalks and wash the leaves carefully. Choose about 20 of the best leaves, arrange a few at a time on a plate and cook on HIGH for about 30 seconds, or until they start to wilt.
5 Lay the leaves on absorbent kitchen paper, pat them dry, then put about a teaspoonful of cooled pate into the centre of each one. Fold in the sides and roll them over to make small parcels and arrange them, seam side down, in a shallow dish. Cover and chill.
6 To serve, spoon over 2 tablespoons of soup, cover and cook the parcels on HIGH for 2 minutes. Have ready bowls of hot chicken soup and carefully lift the parcels into the bowls. (This quantity makes about 20 small parcels).

COURGETTE AND LAMB MOUSSAKAS

Meat

6 courgettes (about 450 g/1 lb)
salt, pepper
1 tbsp oil
2 large onions, finely chopped
300 ml/1/2 pt chicken stock
275 g/10 oz cooked lamb
1 tbsp chopped mint or rosemary
2 egg whites
fresh tomato sauce (see sauces)

1 With a vegetable parer, cut the unpeeled courgettes into long thin slices, put in a dish and cook on HIGH for 2 minutes. Season and leave to cool.
2 To make the onion sauce mixture, cook the chopped onion in the oil on HIGH for 2 minutes. Add 6 tablespoons of stock, cover and cook for 5 minutes or until the onion is soft. Puree the sauce until it is smooth and season well.
3 Mince the lamb with the herbs and add a few tablespoons of stock.
4 To assemble the moussakas, line five 75 ml/3 fl oz ramekins with some of the sliced courgettes, overlapping them slightly to make sure there are no gaps. Spoon in the lamb and press the mixture gently towards the edges, keeping it well inside the sliced courgettes.
5 Whisk the egg whites lightly and fold in half the onion puree. Pour this over the lamb and cover with the remaining courgette slices, tucking in any ends or trimming them with scissors.
6 Arrange the ramekins round the outside of a shallow container or directly on to the ceramic turntable. Cover lightly and cook on MEDIUM for 6 minutes. Leave to stand while you reheat the sauces.
7 Pour the remaining onion sauce and the tomato sauce into separate jugs and reheat on HIGH for 1-2 minutes. Carefully pour off any juices from the moussakas and then turn them over on to large individual plates. Pour the sauces around the side and serve immediately.

GLOBE ARTICHOKES

Parev. Vegetarian

1 globe artichoke per person
lightly salted water

To serve: vinaigrette, lemon sauce or mayonnaise

1 Trim the artichokes with a sharp knife and wash them well. Arrange one or two at a time in a shallow bowl, sprinkle with a few tablespoons of lightly salted water and cover tightly with microwave clingfilm.
2 Cook on HIGH (about 5 minutes for 1 large artichoke, 8-10 minutes for 2), turning the artichokes over after two-thirds of the cooking time. Insert a knife into the base to test if they are done. Leave to cool and then remove the hairy choke from the centre.

BROCCOLI AND CAULIFLOWER WITH CHEESE SAUCE

Milk. Vegetarian

300 ml/1/2 pt cheese sauce (see Wine and Cheese Sauce)
450 g/1 lb broccoli
400 g/14 oz cauliflower
7 tbsp vegetable stock
salt, pepper
50 g/2 oz Dutch cheese, sliced
50 g/2 oz flaked almonds

1 First prepare the cheese sauce, omitting the wine.
2 Separate the broccoli into long florets and the cauliflower into short ones (keep the stalks for soup).
3 Arrange the broccoli with the stalks around the outside of a shallow dish or plate, sprinkle with half the stock and cook, covered, on HIGH for 4 minutes. Season lightly.
4 Cook the cauliflower florets separately with the rest of the stock for about 4 minutes. Sprinkle with salt.
5 Strain the stock into the cheese sauce and pour it over the base of a large round dish. Arrange the broccoli round the edge with the stalks facing inwards. Re-form the cauliflower florets into a 'head' in the centre. Preheat the grill.
6 Arrange the slices of cheese over the vegetables and sprinkle with the almonds. Cook under a hot grill for a few minutes until the cheese is melted and the almonds are brown (take care not to burn them). Serve immediately.

GREEN SALAD WITH HOT BUTTON MUSHROOMS

Milk. Vegetarian

1 large hearty cos lettuce
1 small bunch fresh chives
few parsley sprigs
12 mint leaves
40 g/ 1 1/2 oz salted butter
175 g/6 oz small button mushrooms
3 tbsp olive oil
1 tbsp wine vinegar
salt, pepper

1 Discard the tough outer leaves of the lettuce and wash the rest well. Dry them with paper towels, separating the leaves from the heart rather than cutting them. Arrange the salad in a large bowl.
2 Freshen the herbs in ice cold water and dry them well. Divide them into four piles.
3 Make the dressing by whisking together the oil, vinegar and seasoning. When you are ready to serve the salad, toss the lettuce leaves quickly in the dressing, arrange on four plates and sprinkle over the herbs.
4 In a frying pan (or in the microwave) heat the butter and immediately add the mushrooms, cooking them over high heat for about 2 minutes, or until the juices run. Sprinkle with salt and pepper and immediately spoon the mushrooms over the salads.

CREAM OF JERUSALEM ARTICHOKE SOUP

Milk. Vegetarian

2 tbsp butter
125 g/1/4 lb small mushrooms, sliced
2 onions, chopped
450 g/1 lb Jerusalem artichokes, peeled and sliced
300 ml/1/2 pt vegetable stock
300 ml/1/2 pt milk
salt, pepper

1 Melt the butter in a saucepan and saute the mushrooms for 1 minute. Put them on a plate and then saute the onions and artichokes, adding a little more butter if necessary. Do not let the vegetables brown.
2 Add the stock and bring to the boil. Simmer until the artichokes are cooked, and then taste for seasoning.
3 In a blender or food processor puree the soup, adding the milk slowly.
4 Return the soup to the pan, add the mushrooms and reheat gently, stirring carefully.

SPRING VEGETABLE PLATTER

Parev or Milk. Vegetarian

350 g/12 oz salsify or asparagus
450 g/1 lb courgettes
450 g/1 lb broccoli
juice of 1/2 lemon

To serve: melted butter, vinaigrette or lemon sauce

1 If you are using salsify, prepare it first by peeling the sticks and immediately dropping them into cold water with the lemon juice. Then scrape the asparagus and cut the courgettes and broccoli into even sized pieces.
2 Have ready a heated dish and prepare the sauce you have chosen in advance.
3 In a microwave, cook the vegetables separately on HIGH with a few tablespoons of salted water, (asparagus 5 minutes, salsify 5-7 minutes, courgettes 4 minutes and broccoli 4 minutes), keeping them covered to retain the moisture. Alternatively steam the vegetables over simmering water until they are tender. (Asparagus should stand upright in the water, salsify in it and broccoli and courgettes should be steamed in a basket on the top.)
4 Drain the vegeables, season lightly and pour over the melted butter or lemon sauce if serving hot. Or leave them to cool and serve with vinaigrette.

LEEK AND CUCUMBER SOUP Milk. Vegetarian

450 g/1 lb leeks, sliced
225 g/8 oz potatoes, peeled and diced
500 ml/18 fl oz vegetable stock
15-25 g/1/2 - 1 oz butter
1/2 cucumber, peeled and diced
400 ml/14 fl oz milk
salt, pepper

1 Wash the leeks thoroughly to remove any traces of grit.
2 Put the slices of leek with the diced potatoes into a saucepan and cover with the vegetable stock. Bring to the boil and simmer until tender (about 10 minutes).
3 Pour the soup into a blender and process briefly.
4 Melt the butter in a saucepan, add the cucumber and toss it gently for a few minutes, making sure it does not brown. Add the milk. Pour half the cucumber and milk into the blender and continue processing until the soup is thick. Season well.
5 Pour it back into the saucepan, stirring in the remaining milk and cucumber and reheat gently, stirring constantly, until it is piping hot.

GARDEN VEGETABLE SOUP Milk. Vegetarian

25 g/1 oz salted butter
100 g/4 oz carrots, diced or cut into julienne
4 or 5 spring onions
50 g/2 oz courgettes, sliced
25 g/1 oz mushrooms, sliced
few sticks celery, cut into thin slices
300 ml/ 1/2 pt vegetablestock
300 ml/ 1/2 pt milk
salt, pepper

1 Melt half the butter in a saucepan and saute the carrots, spring onions and courgettes, tossing them with a spoon to make sure they do not brown.
2 Add the rest of the butter and then add the sliced mushrooms and celery. Cook all the vegetables for a few minutes and then pour on the vegetable stock. Bring to the boil and cook for about 5-10 minutes. Season well.
3 Pour in the milk and reheat gently. The soup should not boil again at this stage. Keep warm, stirring occasionally.

CRISPY POTATO SKINS WITH SOUR CREAM AND HERBS Milk. Vegetarian

8 medium sized washed potatoes
2 tbsp oil
coarse salt, pepper
fresh herbs to taste
300 g/12 fl oz sour cream or skimmed milk cheese thinned with a little milk

1 Peel the potatoes thickly, leaving the peeled parts in cold water for another use. Cover the peels with boiling water and boil briskly for five minutes. Drain well.
2 Preheat the grill. Brush a sheet of foil with the oil and arrange the potato skins in a single layer. Sprinkle over some coarse salt and grill for about 10 minutes, turning them over halfway through the cooking time. Make sure they are evenly cooked and crisp.
3 Meanwhile snip the herbs into the sour cream and season with pepper. (Chives are the best but dill or parsley will do.)
4 Drain the potato skins on absorbent paper and serve hot, with the herb cream.

ALMOND, ONION AND MUSHROOM PATE Milk. Vegetarian

25g/1 oz salted butter
1/2 large Spanish onion, finely chopped
75 g/3 oz mushrooms, finely chopped
salt, pepper
2 tbsp chopped fresh parsley
50 g/2 oz ground almonds

1 Melt the butter in a frying pan and immediately add the chopped onion. Stir over low heat for a few minutes until the onion begins to soften.
2 Add the mushrooms and continue cooking until the juices begin to run. Season well and then mix in the parsley and ground almonds. Taste for seasoning and spoon the mixture into very small pots. Serve cool.

AUBERGINE DIP Parev. Vegetarian

2 aubergines
3-4 tbsp olive oil
2 cloves garlic, crushed
1/2 onion, chopped
juice of 1/2 lemon
pinch sugar, salt, pepper

To serve: Vegetable crudites (carrot, celery, peppers)

1 Prick the aubergines in several places and cook in a hot oven until they are soft (about 30 minutes). Alternatively microwave on HIGH for about 4-6 minutes.
2 Heat half the oil in a pan and saute the garlic and onion over low heat for about 3 minutes, stirring until they are soft.
3 Cut the aubergine in half, discard the seeds and scoop out the flesh. Puree this in a blender with the onion mixture, gradually adding the remaining oil, seasoning and lemon juice.
4 When the mixture is smooth, cool it quickly and then cover with clingfilm to stop it discolouring.

COURGETTE AND YELLOW PEPPERS AU GRATIN Milk. Vegetarian

275 g/10oz courgettes
2 medium sized yellow peppers, de-seeded
3-4 tbsp olive oil
salt, pepper
75 g/3 oz Dutch cheese, thinly sliced

1 Cut the courgettes into sticks and slice the peppers into long strips.
2 Heat half the oil in a frying pan and saute the courgettes briefly, turning them frequently so that they do not brown. Add the rest of the oil and the pepper strips and continue cooking for about 3 minutes. The vegetables should be crisp. Season well.
3 Transfer the courgettes and peppers to an ovenproof dish. Arrange the thinly sliced cheese in a lattice pattern over the top and cook under a preheated hot grill for a few minutes until the cheese is bubbling. Serve immediately.

Note: If you prefer the vegetables to be well done, complete the cooking in a preheated moderate oven for about half an hour instead of the grill.

POTATO SOUP

Milk. Vegetarian

3 large carrots
2 leeks
1 onion
2 stalks celery

25 g/1 oz butter
3 medium sized potatoes
300 ml/1/2 pt milk
salt, pepper

1 First make a vegetable stock with 1 1/2 carrots, 1 1/2 leeks, 1/2 onion and the celery. Place them all in a pan, cover with water and bring to the boil. Leave simmering for 1/2 to 1 hour. Drain, reserving the stock and discarding the vegetables. This should make about 425 ml/3/4 pt stock. (Alternatively use 1 flat tablespoon of vegetable stock powder in the same amount of boiling water.)
2 Shred the remaining onion, leek and carrot into julienne strips and saute them in the butter. Cook the potatoes in salted water until they are soft and drain well.
3 Put the potatoes, milk and stock into a blender or through a sieve until the mixture is a smooth puree (do not overblend or the mixture will become gluey). Check the seasoning, add the vegetable strips and reheat gently, stirring, until hot.

TOMATO AND RED PEPPER SOUP

Parev or Milk. Vegetarian

5 large tomatoes
2-4 tbsp oil
1 onion, chopped
450 g/1 lb red peppers, de-seeded and sliced

2 tbsp tomato puree
450 ml/ 3/4 pt vegetable stock
salt, pepper, pinch sugar

To serve: Sour cream (optional) sprigs of dill

1 Peel the tomatoes by plunging them into boiling water for half a minute. The skins will then come off easily. Chop them, reserving the juice.
2 Heat half the oil in a frying pan and saute the chopped onion over medium heat until it softens but does not brown. Add the peppers and continue cooking with the rest of the oil for about five minutes.
3 Stir in the tomatoes, tomato puree and a few tablespoons of stock and continue cooking until the vegetables are tender. Then blend the mixture with the remaining stock and seasoning until it is smooth. Pass the soup through a strainer to remove the pepper skins, taste again for seasoning and serve either hot or chilled. (If you use a mouli-legumes instead of a blender you won't need to strain the soup.)

ASPARAGUS AND EGG SALAD

Parev. Vegetarian

500 g/1 lb fresh asparagus
3 hard-boiled eggs
3 spring onions, sliced
4 radishes, diced
5 cm/2 in piece cucumber, diced
12 cherry tomatoes
salt, pepper

1 Boil the asparagus until tender (alternatively microwave on HIGH with 3-4 tablespoons of water for about 5 minutes). Drain and leave to cool.
2 Chop the eggs finely and mix with the spring onions, radishes and cucumber, and pile the mixture in the centre of a dish. Surround with the asparagus and garnish with the cherry tomatoes.

CHILLED ONION SOUP

Meat

2 large onions
outer leaves from a large lettuce
350 ml/12 fl oz chicken stock (or 1 stock cube dissolved in same amount of water)
3 medium sized potatoes, cooked
4 tbsp parev milk powder
1/2 tsp sugar
salt, pepper
3-4 spring onions, finely chopped

1 Peel and slice the onions and put them in a saucepan with the lettuce leaves and half the chicken stock. Cook until the onions are soft.
2 Put the cooked potatoes and the rest of the chicken stock into a blender and process briefly (not too long otherwise the mixture becomes gluey). Add the onion mixture and the parev milk powder and continue blending until the mixture is smooth. Season well. Add a little more stock or water if the soup is too thick.
3 Sprinkle with the chopped spring onions and serve chilled.

CHILLED ONION SOUP

Milk. Vegetarian

Proceed as above but use 300 ml/1/2 pt vegetable stock to cook the onions. Puree the cooked potatoes with the cooked onion mixture and then add 300 ml/1/2 pt warm milk until smooth.

COURGETTE AND ALMOND SOUP

Meat

700 g/1 1/2 lbs courgettes, trimmed
725 ml/1 1/4 pts chicken stock
2 tbsp oil
1 large onion, chopped
salt, pepper
150 ml/1/4 pt parev milk or cream
2 oz ground almonds
50 g/2 oz toasted slivered almonds

1 Cut one courgette into thin slivers and curl into coils, securing with a cocktail stick. Poach in a little chicken stock and set aside for garnish.
2 Heat the oil in a large pan and saute the chopped onion, stirring frequently so that it does not brown. Chop the remaining courgettes and add them to the oil and saute until they are beginning to soften. Pour in the remaining stock and cook over low heat until the vegetables are tender. Season well.
3 Puree the soup in a blender, gradually adding the parev milk and the ground almonds. When it is smooth, reheat it gently and serve in bowls. Slide the courgette curls off the cocktail sticks, and spoon into the soup with the toasted almonds.

COURGETTE AND ALMOND SOUP

Milk. Vegetarian

Proceed as above, using vegetable stock, butter and fresh milk instead of the chicken stock, oil and parev milk.

FRIED CHICKEN PICK-UPS — Meat

225 g/8 oz raw chicken
1-2 eggs, beaten
salt, pepper
75 g/3 oz matzo meal, medium ground
oil for frying

1 Cut the chicken into finger-length pieces, dip each one into beaten egg and then coat with the seasoned matzo meal.
2 Heat the oil in a deep pan and fry the chicken pieces for about 10 minutes, or until they are golden brown. Serve immediately or reheat on a baking sheet in a hot oven, Gas 6, 400F, 200C. (These amounts make about thirty pieces.)

BABY ONIONS IN SPICY TOMATO SAUCE — Parev. Vegetarian

36 baby onions
300 ml/10 fl oz dry white wine
160 ml/6 fl oz olive oil
1 tbsp wine vinegar
1 garlic clove, crushed
fresh herbs (oregano or thyme)
salt, pepper
2 tbsp tomato puree
125 g/4 oz raisins

1 Place the onions in a bowl and pour over some boiling water. Leave for a few minutes and then peel. (The skins should be easier to remove now.)
2 Put the onions in a heavy saucepan with the wine, oil, wine vinegar, garlic and a few fresh herbs. Bring to the boil, season and simmer until the onions are tender (about 15 minutes). Stir in the tomato puree and the raisins and cook on low heat for another minute. Leave to cool.

RED PEPPER SALAD — Parev. Vegetarian

2 small onions, thinly sliced
olive oil for frying
3 red peppers, de-seeded and thinly sliced
5 ripe tomatoes, peeled and roughly chopped
2 cloves garlic, crushed
salt, pepper, 1 1/2 tsp sugar

1 Saute the onions in a little olive oil in a frying pan. When they are soft but not brown add the peppers and saute, over medium heat, for a few minutes, stirring frequently.
2 Add the tomatoes, garlic and seasoning and continue cooking for about 10 minutes. Leave to cool.

GRAVLAX - PICKLED SALMON — Parev or Milk

(Start 2 days in advance)

900 g/2 lbs fresh salmon or salmon trout
25g/1 oz sugar
25 g/1 oz coarse salt
15 crushed peppercorns
sprigs fresh dill

To serve : Fresh dill, sour cream, (optional)

1 Cut the fish in half lengthwise and remove the backbone carefully. Mix the sugar, salt and pepper and rub this seasoning into both sides of the two fillets. Cover with the dill, wrap in clingfilm and refrigerate for two days, turning them over occasionally.
2 Scrape off the dill mixture, slice the salmon downwards into 1/4 inch slices and arrange on a decorative plate. Serve with extra fresh dill.

MAIN COURSES

NAVARIN OF LAMB (SPRING LAMB CASSEROLE) — Meat

450 ml/3/4 pt chicken or lamb stock
900 g/2 lbs shoulder of lamb, boned
8 small onions
625 g/1 lb 6 oz small new potatoes
450 g/1 lb small new carrots
12 tiny mauve-tipped white turnips
1 clove garlic, crushed
large sprig fresh rosemary
1 tsp sugar, salt, pepper

1. Use the bones from the lamb to make a stock or use chicken stock. (A cube can be used but may drown the delicate flavour of the vegetables.)
2. Dice the meat and saute it in a non-stick frying pan over fairly high heat until the fat starts to run. Add the small onions and cook until both start to brown. Transfer to a microwave casserole.
3. Put the potatoes in a dish with 150 ml/1/4 pt boiling water and cook on HIGH for five minutes. Drain and set aside.
4. Pour the stock into the frying pan, bring it to the boil and deglaze the pan (stir in any fragments that are adhering to the sides of the pan).
5. Mix the carrots and turnips with the meat and add the garlic, rosemary, sugar and seasoning. Pour over half the stock, cover and cook on HIGH for 15 minutes, then on LOW for 3O minutes. Add the potatoes and the rest of the stock and continue cooking on LOW for 7 minutes or until the lamb is tender.

PEPPERS STUFFED WITH MINCED BEEF — Meat

450 g/1 lb minced lean beef
1-2 tbsp oil
1 onion
2 sticks celery
50 g/2 oz button mushrooms
pinch cinnamon
salt, black pepper
4 red peppers
2 tbsp olive oil

1. Saute the minced beef in a non-stick pan for a few minutes, stirring until it is brown. Transfer it to a microwave casserole.
2. Saute the chopped onion and celery in the oil until they are golden and then add the mushrooms. Season well and when the juices are beginning to run pour the vegetables into the minced beef in the casserole.
3. Cover and cook on LOW for about 10-15 minutes or until the beef is tender.
4. Cut the tops off the peppers and remove the seeds. Wash and shake dry. Microwave on HIGH for 2-3 minutes.
5. Fill the peppers with the meat mixture, arrange them on a shallow dish, spooning any extra meat into the centre. Replace the tops of the peppers, drizzle over the olive oil and microwave on HIGH for 3-4 minutes.

SALMON IN SPINACH PARCELS

Milk

1.4 kg/3 lbs salmon or salmon trout, skinned and filleted
25 g/1 oz butter
1 tbsp chopped fresh dill
grated rind of 1 lemon
salt, pepper
225-450 g/8 oz - 1 lb fresh spinach (large leaves)

1. Trim the salmon into eight 7.5 cm/3 in squares and remove all the bones.
2. Mix the butter with the dill, lemon rind, salt and pepper.
3. Wash the spinach well, drain it and then choose 8 of the best shaped large leaves. Remove the stalks and cook on HIGH for 30 seconds to soften them.
4. Arrange the spinach on a layer of absorbent kitchen paper, press over another layer to absorb any moisture and then season the leaves lightly.
5. Place a salmon square on each leaf and spread over some of the butter mixture. Fold over the spinach to make a neat envelope, then arrange them with the joins downwards in a shallow round dish.
6. Cover and cook on HIGH for 4 minutes. If the butter oozes out, brush it over the top of the spinach before serving.

COOL HALIBUT SALAD

Parev

550 g/1 1/4 lbs halibut, skinned and filleted
50ml/2 fl oz white wine
225 g/8 oz asparagus tips
3 tbsp vegetable stock or water
1 crisp lettuce, such as Webb's or oakleaf
12 cherry tomatoes
75g/3 oz small button mushrooms
1 clove garlic, crushed
6 tbsp olive oil
2 tbsp wine vinegar
salt, pepper

1. Cut the halibut into large chunks or cubes, put in a dish and pour over the wine. Leave to stand while preparing the vegetables.
2. Arrange the asparagus tips on a plate, sprinkle with a few tablespoons of lightly salted water and cook on HIGH for 3-4 minutes, covered.
3. Wash and dry the salad leaves, tomatoes and mushrooms.
4. Mix the garlic and oil in a small jar and cook on HIGH for 20 seconds. Leave to cool slightly then add the wine vinegar and seasoning. Shake the dressing very well.
5. Cover the fish and cook on HIGH for 1 minute, stir and cook again for another minute, or until it is opaque. Drain and leave to cool.
6. To assemble the salad, place the leaves on a large dish with the cooled fish in the centre. Arrange the drained asparagus, mushrooms and tomatoes around the fish and strain the dressing over the salad immediately before you serve it.

CUCUMBER,DILL AND FISH SALAD

Milk

2 large cucumbers
1 spring onion, chopped
small bunch fresh dill
salt, pepper
75 ml/3 fl oz milk
500 g/1 1/4lbs fresh cod fillet, skinned
1 bunch watercress, trimmed
2 crisp apples
4 tbsp mayonnaise
2 tbsp natural yogurt

1. Skin one of the cucumbers and cut it into dice. Sprinkle it with salt and leave to drain on absorbent paper to remove some of the moisture.
2. Put the fish in a pan with the milk, spring onion and half the dill. Season well and poach gently until the fish begins to flake. Drain and remove the herbs and then leave the fish to cool.
3. Wash and drain the cucumber cubes and dry well. Slice the remaining cucumber thinly.
4. Just before serving slice the apples and mix them with mayonnaise, yogurt and diced cucumber. Gently mix in the flaked fish and spoon the mixture into the centre of a large dish. Arrange the cucumber slices round the edge and garnish with the remaining sprigs of dill.

AUBERGINES WITH TOMATOES AND CHEESE

Milk. Vegetarian

550 g/1 1/4lbs aubergines (2 large or 4 small)
salt, pepper
6-8 tbsp oil
1/2 onion, finely chopped
1 clove garlic, crushed
450 g/1 lb soft tomatoes, skinned and chopped
1/2 tsp sugar
225 g/8 oz Dutch cheese, sliced thinly

1. Cut the aubergines in half lengthwise and scoop out some of the flesh. Sprinkle the shells and flesh with salt and leave to drain for at least 30 minutes on absorbent kitchen paper.
2. Rinse in cold water, drain well and pat dry. Chop the flesh into cubes.
3. Heat half the oil in a frying pan and saute the aubergine shells first, pressing them down slightly to make sure both sides are cooked. Then transfer them to an ovenproof dish. Preheat the oven or grill.
4. Heat the rest of the oil and fry the onion and garlic until golden brown. Add the aubergine cubes and fry for a few more minutes. Stir in the chopped tomatoes, turning up the heat to reduce the amount of juice. Season with salt, pepper and sugar.
5. Spoon the filling into the shells and cover with the sliced cheese. Then either grill or bake the stuffed aubergines in a hot oven (Gas 6, 400F, 200C) until the cheese is melted and the filling is quite hot.

PASSOVER BAGEL PIZZAS

Milk. Vegetarian

150 ml/5 fl oz water
75 ml/2 1/2 fl oz oil
100 gm/ 4 oz matzo meal
1 tbsp sugar
3 eggs
1/4 tsp salt
for the topping : tomato sauce (see sauces)
about 100 g/3-4 oz grated cheese

1 Put the water, oil, sugar and salt into a saucepan. Bring to the boil and continue cooking over high heat while you gradually stir in the matzo meal. Preheat the oven to Gas 5, 375F, 190C.
2 Remove from the heat and beat in the eggs, one at a time.
3 With wet hands form the mixture into balls of about 2 inches diameter and place them on a greased baking sheet. If the mixture is too soft, add a little more matzo meal. Press a hole in the middle of each one.
4 Bake for about 35 minutes or until the bagels are brown.
5 Meanwhile prepare the sauce and the cheese for the topping.
6 When the bagels are cooked slice them in half horizontally, spoon over some of the sauce and top with a generous amount of grated cheese.
7 Return to the oven or grill until the cheese is melted and the bagels are heated through.

Note: This amount makes about 12 bagels. Without the topping they can be eaten fresh with butter or jam, but are not good cold.

CHEESE OMELETTES WITH SOFT BUTTERED ONIONS

Milk. Vegetarian

(Serves 2)

2 tbsp oil
2 onions, finely chopped
100 g/4 oz butter
50 ml/2 fl oz cream
100 g/4 oz hard cheese, grated
6 eggs
salt, pepper

1 First make the filling. Heat the oil in a frying pan and add the chopped onions. Stir over low heat, adding some of the butter and stirring so that the onions do not brown. When they are soft, stir in the cream and half of the grated cheese. Season well and pour into a dish.
2 Whisk the eggs in a bowl with 2 tablespoons of water, salt and pepper.
3 Melt 15 g/1/2 oz butter in an omelette pan and when it begins to foam pour in half the eggs. (Have ready heated plates as the omelettes are made one at a time.) Cook gently until the bottom of the omelette is just beginning to set. Lift the edges with a palette knife so that the uncooked egg pours out to the sides. Shake the pan, working quickly so that the omelette is not too firm.
4 Spoon half the onion mixture over the omelette and lift one side over the top. Slide it out on to the heated plate and keep it warm while you make the other omelette.
5 Spread any remaining butter over the finished omelettes and sprinkle with the rest of the cheese.

VEAL OR TURKEY IN WHITE ONION SAUCE — Meat

4 veal chops or turkey schnitzels
3 large onions
600 ml/1 pt veal or chicken stock
2 tbsp oil or margarine
salt, pepper

1 Saute the veal chops in the oil or margarine in a large frying pan. Cook them for about 5 minutes each side, when they will be slightly coloured. (Turkey schnitzels will take less time as they are thinner.) Transfer them to an ovenproof dish.
2 Slice the onions thickly and cook them briefly in the frying pan in any fat that remains (adding a little more if necessary). Pour over the stock and bring it to the boil, stirring well to deglaze the pan with the meat juices. Cover and simmer until the onions are very soft.
3 Pass the cooked onions through a sieve or blend to make a thick puree. Pour the puree over the chops, season well and cover.
4 Cook the chops or schnitzels in a moderate oven (Gas 4, 350F, 180C) until they are tender. The chops will take about 40 minutes, turkey about 20.
5 Serve hot with green vegetables and new potatoes.

CHICKEN WITH AUBERGINES — Meat

2 kg/5 lbs roasting chicken
5 large tomatoes, peeled and chopped
1 clove garlic, crushed
2 aubergines, peeled and cubed
2 onions, sliced
2 tbsp oil
75ml/3 fl oz dry white wine
salt, pepper, sugar

1 Preheat the oven (to Gas 7, 425F, 22OC) and roast the chicken for about an hour. After about 30 minutes add the tomatoes and garlic and baste the chicken with this mixture.
2 While it is cooking prepare the aubergines. Sprinkle salt over the slices and leave them to drain in a colander for about 30 minutes. Then wash and drain them to get rid of any bitter juices. Dry them well.
3 Saute the onion and the aubergine pieces in the oil until they are crisp and brown.
4 When the chicken is cooked, carve it into portions. Pour off any fat from the pan juices and stir the wine into the pan. Season to taste, add a little sugar and then sieve this sauce over the chicken. Cover with the aubergine and onion mixture and serve very hot.

BRAISED BEEF — Meat

1.5-1.75 kg/3-4 lbs rolled brisket or top rib
2 onions, sliced
2 carrots, sliced
3 sticks celery
1/2 beef stock cube
salt, pepper

1 Cut a large sheet of foil and place the meat in the centre. Cover with the sliced onions and carrots and place the celery at the side. Sprinkle over the crumbled stock cube, season with salt and pepper and cover with the foil to make a parcel. Stand this in a casserole.
2 Cook the beef in a moderate oven (Gas 4, 350F, 180C) for about 3 hours. Pour the juices into a bowl and remove the fat. Slice the beef and pour the juices over it as a gravy.

HALIBUT IN EGG AND LEMON SAUCE

Parev

1 small onion
300 ml/1/2 pt water
1 tsp sugar
salt, pepper
4 halibut steaks
3-4 egg yolks
juice of 2 lemons (reserve a few slices for decoration)

1 Slice the onion into a large shallow pan, cover with the water and seasoning and bring to the boil. Simmer for about 10 minutes and then carefully lower in the halibut steaks. Cook over a low heat for about 10 minutes and then remove the fish with a slotted spoon to a serving dish.
2 Reduce the cooking liquid over high heat for a few minutes.
3 Beat the egg yolks with the lemon juice and pour on the strained fish liquid. Return the sauce to the pan and stir carefully over very low heat, taking great care not to let it boil. When the sauce thickens remove it immediately and pour it over the fish. Leave to cool and garnish with slices of fresh lemon.

GRILLED TROUT WITH TOMATOES AND MUSHROOMS

Parev or Milk

4 large trout
4 tomatoes, halved
175 g/6 oz button mushrooms
3 tbsp oil or butter
sprigs of fresh dill, chives or chervil
salt, pepper

1 Wash and dry the fish and arrange them on a grill pan or a sheet of lightly oiled foil. Season well and brush with a little oil or butter.
2 Make some deep cuts in the tomato halves. Chop up some of the herbs and press about 2 tablespoons into the cut tomatoes. Season with salt and pepper and arrange the tomatoes around the fish.
3 Grill the trout for about 5 minutes each side or until the skin is lightly browned and crisp.
4 While it is grilling, saute the mushrooms in the remaining oil or butter in a small frying pan. Serve the fish on heated plates garnished with the herbed tomatoes and button mushrooms.

TO COOK A WHOLE SALMON

Parev

2-3 kg/5-6 lbs fresh salmon
1 lemon
salt, pepper
2 tbsp oil

To serve: Slices of cucumber

1 Place the fish in the centre of an oiled piece of foil. Put a few slices of lemon inside the fish and arrange the rest on the top with the seasoning. Sprinkle over the oil and wrap up the foil to make a loose parcel.
2 Cook the salmon in a preheated oven (Gas 7, 425F, 22OC) for about 15 minutes and then turn the oven off. Leave the fish in the foil parcel in the oven until it is quite cold, when it will be just cooked and none of the juices will be lost.
3 Remove the skin and lemon and garnish with slices of cucumber.

CHICKEN BREASTS WITH BURNT ALMOND STUFFING — Meat

(Serves 2)

1 tbsp oil
2 tbsp flaked or sliced almonds
2 fat spring onions, sliced
1 carrot, finely chopped
small stick celery, sliced
1/2 chicken stock cube
3 tbsp medium matzo meal
2 breasts of chicken with the skin

1. Heat the oil in a small frying pan and fry the almonds until they are turning brown. Remove them with a slotted spoon and then saute the chopped onions, carrot and celery for a few minutes.
2. Make up the stock cube with 150 ml/1/4 pt boiling water and pour half the stock over the vegetables. Cook over high heat until the liquid has been reduced and the vegetables are just moist. Mix in the matzo meal and nuts.
3. Remove the skin from the chicken breasts and set aside. Arrange the chicken in a shallow dish, pour on the remaining stock, cover and microwave on HIGH for about 4 1/2 minutes. Test to see if they are done by inserting a sharp knife into the centre.
4. Put a sheet of foil on the grill pan and preheat the grill. Drain the chicken breasts and lay them on the foil. Spoon over the almond stuffing and then cover with the skins, being careful to enclose the stuffing.
5. Grill the stuffed chicken breasts about 3 inches from the heat for about 10-15 minutes. The skin should be brown and crisp. Transfer to heated plates and serve with a green vegetable or salad.

AUBERGINES WITH LAMB — Meat

4 small aubergines, total weight 575 g/1 1/4 lbs
450 g/1 lb shoulder of lamb, cubed
3 tbsp olive oil
2 onions, quartered
2 cloves garlic, crushed
150 ml/1/4 pt beef stock
1 tbsp chopped fresh coriander
salt, pepper

1. First prepare the aubergines. Cut them in half, sprinkle with salt and leave for about 30 minutes. Wash and drain the halves and then cut out the centres, leaving the shells. Dice the aubergine flesh and put it with the shells into a covered microwave dish. Cook on HIGH for 2 minutes.
2. In a frying pan saute the aubergine shells and cubes in some of the oil and when they are brown remove with a slotted spoon.
3. Saute the lamb cubes over high heat until they start to brown and release some fat. Pour in the remaining oil, add the onions and garlic and cook until both the lamb and onions are brown. Season well, pour over the beef stock and deglaze the pan (stir in any fragments that are adhering to the sides of the pan).
4. Transfer the meat and onions, with the stock, to a dish, cover and cook on MEDIUM for 15 minutes. Add the cubed aubergine and continue cooking on LOW for about 10 minutes or until the meat is tender.
5. Spoon the mixture into the aubergine shells, reheat for a few minutes and sprinkle with chopped coriander.

NOTES

TROUT IN WINE

Parev or Milk

(Serves 2)

2 large pink trout (about 550 g/1 1/4 lbs)
3 tbsp white wine
salt, pepper

To serve: Melted butter, lemon sauce or wine and cheese sauce

1 Remove the heads and dry the fish well. Sprinkle salt and pepper inside and over the top of the trout.
2 Arrange them in a shallow oval dish with the thickest parts nearest to the outside. Pour over the wine and cook on HIGH covered, for 4 minutes, turning them over halfway. Leave to stand for a few minutes, remove the skin and serve with any of the above sauces.

SEA BASS WITH GINGER, SPRING ONIONS AND SHERRY

Parev

1.25 kg/2 1/2 lbs sea bass
2.5 cm/1 in piece ginger root, peeled and sliced
3 large spring onions, chopped
3 tbsp medium sherry
salt, pepper

1 Make two or three slashes in each side of the skin and curl the fish to fit a round or oval dish. Sprinkle over the ginger and onions, pour on the sherry, cover and cook on HIGH for about 6 minutes, turning the fish over once during the cooking time. Leave to stand for a few minutes.
2 Lift off the skin, season the fish lightly and strain over the sauce.

BEEF SALAD

Meat

550 g/1 1/4 lbs potatoes, diced
100 g/4 oz carrots, cut into sticks or diced
225 g/8 oz courgettes, cut into sticks
450 g/1 lb cooked roast beef or rare grilled steak, cooled and cubed
150 ml/1/4 pt mayonnaise

1 Cover the potatoes with boiling water and cook on HIGH for about 8 minutes. Cook the carrots and courgettes separately with a few tablespoons of water on HIGH for 3 minutes each. Drain the vegetables and leave to cool.
2 Mix the cooked beef with the vegetables and mayonnaise.

STUFFED CABBAGE LEAVES

Meat

1 winter green cabbage (about 16 leaves)
1 tbsp oil
1 onion, chopped
350 g/12 oz cooked chicken or minced beef mixture (see Stuffed pepper recipe)
6 tbsp gravy or chicken stock
25g/1 oz almonds or hazelnuts
salt, pepper

1 Cut a cone out of the base of the cabbage so that the leaves come away and wash them very well. Shake off most of the water and cook half at a time on HIGH for about 1-2 minutes, or until they have softened slightly. Drain and pat dry.
2 Heat the oil in a small saucepan and saute the chopped onion over high heat. After a few minutes add the nuts and toss together until the onion and nuts are golden brown.
3 Cut the chicken into very small pieces and moisten with a few tablespoons of stock or gravy or alternatively use minced beef which has been cooked as in the recipe for Stuffed Peppers.
4 Lay out the cabbage leaves and put a heaped spoonful of the chicken or meat mixture into each one. Roll them up into neat parcels, folding in the edges and making sure the filling is completely enclosed. Arrange them fairly close in a single layer in a shallow dish.
5 Sprinkle the remaining stock or gravy over the cabbage rolls. Cover and cook on HIGH for about 3 minutes or until they are very hot. Serve with boiled or mashed potatoes.

NOTES

SPANISH CHICKEN — Meat

2kg/5 lbs roasting chicken, jointed
2 large red peppers, de-seeded and sliced
1 onion, sliced
1 clove garlic, crushed
oil for frying
3 ripe tomatoes, peeled
1 tsp sugar, salt, pepper

1. Saute the chicken joints in a non-stick frying pan until some of the fat begins to run and the skin starts to brown. Turn them over and after a few more minutes transfer them to an ovenproof dish or casserole. Preheat the oven to Gas 5, 375F, 190C.
2. Fry the peppers, onion and garlic in the fat remaining in the pan, adding a little oil if necessary. Cook until the onion just starts to colour, then pour the vegetables over the chicken.
3. Put the chopped tomatoes in the frying pan with a little water and sugar. Stir over high heat for a few minutes, season and then pour the tomato mixture round the chicken joints. (You can prepare the dish in advance up to this point.)
4. Cook, covered, for about an hour, removing the lid for the last 15 minutes if you like the chicken and peppers to be slightly brown.

TURKEY SCHNITZELS WITH LEMON — Meat

680 g/1 1/2lbs turkey slices, cut very thin from the breast
2 tbsp fine matzo meal
salt, pepper
3 eggs, beaten
225 g/8 oz medium matzo meal
oil for frying
lemon wedges for garnishing

1. Pound the slices until they are very thin and then toss them in the fine meal. Sprinkle with salt and pepper and also season the beaten eggs.
2. Dip the schnitzels first in the beaten egg then in the medium matzo meal.
3. Heat enough oil to cover the base of a shallow frying pan and when it is hot fry the schnitzels for about 5 minutes on each side, or until they are golden brown. Put them on a serving dish in a warm oven until you have finished frying them all. Garnish with wedges of lemon.

CHICKEN LIVERS WITH STIR-FRIED VEGETABLES — Meat

350 g/12 oz chicken livers
2 tbsp oil
75 g/3 oz mushrooms, sliced
75 g/3 oz spring onions, chopped
100 g/4 oz Chinese leaves, shredded
2 carrots, thinly sliced diagonally
salt, pepper
2 tbsp sherry

1. Grill the livers on a rack until they are cooked and keep warm on a heated dish.
2. Heat the oil in a frying pan and saute the mushrooms, onions and carrots and then add the Chinese leaves. Season well, tossing the vegetables very briefly so they are still crisp. Mix them with the livers and sprinkle over the sherry.

ROAST RACKS OF LAMB WITH ROAST POTATOES

Meat

3 racks of lamb (4 trimmed chops on each)
4 large potatoes
1-2 cloves garlic, peeled and halved
1 large sprig fresh rosemary
2-3 tbsp oil
salt, pepper

1 Place the lamb on a rack in a roasting tin. Preheat the oven to Gas 7, 425F, 220C.
2 Peel the potatoes and cut them into fairly small pieces. Boil for about 5 minutes in lightly salted water and then drain.
3 Put the oil in an ovenproof dish with the garlic pieces and rosemary. Add the potatoes and turn them round to coat with the oil. Roast for about an hour, turning them over halfway to brown both sides.
4 After 30 minutes put in the lamb and cook on a high shelf for 15 minutes. Season with salt and pepper and continue cooking for a further 15 minutes.
5 Have ready heated dishes and plates. Cut through the racks of lamb and serve three chops to each person with the roast potatoes on the side. The lamb will be slightly pink. If you prefer well done lamb allow slightly longer cooking time.

GRILLED DUCK BREASTS

Meat

4 boneless duck breasts
2 tbsp clear honey
8 tbsp dry sherry
1/4 tsp ginger
salt, pepper

To serve: Poached apricots, apples or apricot puree (see sauces)

1 First make the marinade. Mix together the honey, sherry, ginger and seasoning. With a sharp knife, make diamond patterns on the duck skin by cutting three or four lines in two directions (this is to stop the skin curling). Leave the duck breasts in the marinade for a few hours.
2 Preheat the grill to high and drain the duck breasts, reserving the marinade.
3 Arrange the duck with the skin side on a rack and grill for 5 minutes. Turn the breast over, brush with the remaining marinade and continue grilling until the duck is tender. (After about 15-20 minutes the skin will be crisp and the meat will be slightly pink. For well done meat cook a bit longer but it becomes tougher the longer it is cooked.)
4 Serve the duck with poached fruit or fruit puree and a tossed green salad.

ROAST DUCK

Meat

2 ducks (whole, or with breasts removed)
salt, pepper

To serve: Sliced oranges or apple sauce

1 Preheat the oven to Gas 7, 425F, 220C. Arrange the ducks, breast side down, on a rack over a roasting tin. Prick the skin in several places with a fork. Roast the ducks for 30 minutes and then pour off the fat.
2 Turn the oven down to Gas 5, 375F, 190C. Continue roasting the ducks for a further hour, pouring off the fat every 20 minutes. Season well, turn the ducks over (if you have removed the breasts, cover the tops with pieces of foil). Continue cooking for another half hour. Carve them into portions and keep warm on a heated dish.
3 Deglaze the roasting dish with a little water or chicken stock, bring to the boil and pour this gravy into a heated sauceboat.

DESSERTS AND SAUCES

ALMOND PETIT FOURS

Parev

230 g/8 oz ground almonds
115 g/4 oz icing sugar, sifted
2 egg whites
1 tbsp oil

1 Grease a baking tin with the oil and preheat the oven to Gas 7, 425F, 220C.
2 Mix the ground almonds with the icing sugar. Whisk the egg whites until they are stiff and then mix in just enough to form a fairly firm mixture. (If it is too soft the biscuits will lose their shape.)
3 Pipe the mixture into rosettes on to the baking tin or alternatively form it into small balls. Bake for about 10 minutes or until the tops are just starting to brown.
4 Slide a palette knife underneath the petit fours and remove them carefully from the tin while they are still hot. They will be slightly soft but will harden a little as they cool. Store in a covered container or freeze.

Note: This amount makes about 30 biscuits.

BUTTER NUT CAKE

Milk

175 g/6 oz unsalted butter
125 g/4 oz sugar
4 eggs
175 g/6 oz ground almonds or hazelnuts
5 tbsp/2 1/4 oz potato flour

1 Grease a 7 inch cake tin and line the base (or use one with a loose bottom). Preheat the oven to Gas 4, 350F, 180C.
2 Soften the butter slightly and then mix it with the sugar. Beat in the eggs, one at a time, adding a few of the ground nuts after each one. Fold in the remaining nuts and potato flour. Pour the mixture into the prepared tin and bake for about 40-45 minutes.

RED FRUIT SALAD

Parev

250 g/8 oz mixed berries (raspberries, blackberries, red or black currants)
8 ripe plums
8 ripe apricots
1-3 tbsp sugar
250 g/8 oz seedless grapes

1 Mix the berries with the sugar. Cut the plums and apricots into pieces and put half of them in a pan with the berries.
2 Cook over very low heat with a little water until the fruit is just beginning to soften and the juices are starting to run.
3 Leave to cool slightly, add the grapes and the rest of the fruit. Taste for sweetness and leave to get cold.

Note: This can be made with frozen berries, but they should be defrosted first before cooking with the other fruit.

TOMATO SAUCE

Parev. Vegetarian

225 g/1/2 lb onions, finely chopped
1 tbsp oil
450 g/1 lb tomatoes, peeled and chopped
1 tsp sugar
salt, pepper

1 Saute the chopped onion in a little oil and stir until it is slightly golden. Add the tomatoes, sugar, salt and pepper and cook over low heat for about 15 minutes.
2 If you like a smooth sauce, strain the mixture. Otherwise mash it slightly.

LEMON SAUCE

Meat or Parev. Vegetarian

2 egg yolks
juice of 1/2 lemon
75 ml/3 fl oz light vegetable or chicken stock, heated
salt, pepper

1 Beat the egg yolks with the lemon juice in a bowl. Pour on the hot stock, season and pour into a pan.
2 Cook the sauce over low heat, stirring constantly until it thickens slightly. Take care that it does not boil otherwise it will curdle. (If it does, remove it at once, stir in a few ice cubes and whisk vigorously. If it is still not right, start again with another egg yolk and gradually whisk in the curdled mixture, very slowly.)
3 Remove from the heat and serve immediately.

KUMQUAT PRESERVE FOR COLD MEATS

Parev

125 g/4 oz kumquats
2 tsp sugar

1 Cut the kumquats in half and remove any visible pips. Put them in a small pan with 4 teaspoons of water and the sugar and bring to the boil.
2 Cook on low heat for about 5 minutes or until the kumquats are soft and the juice has become syrupy.
3 Leave the kumquats to cool slightly, remove any more pips you can see and pour the preserve into a small pot.
4 Serve with cold beef, tongue or chicken or with hot roast duck.

Note : The preserve also freezes well.

MELON WITH FRESH ORANGE JELLY Parev

1 large honeydew melon or 2 small ogen melons
juice of 3-4 oranges
3-4 tbsp kosher gelatin

1 First prepare the gelatin (4 tbsp if you like the jelly to be quite firm). Mix the powder with a few spoonfuls of orange juice in a small cup. Place the cup in a pan of hot water and stir over gentle heat for a few minutes until the gelatin mixture softens. Then use it, either hot to pour into a hot mixture, or cold into a cold one, stirring well all the time to avoid stringiness.
2 Cut the flesh of the melon into dice or balls and place in a bowl. Pour the juice into a measuring jug together with the strained juice of the oranges.
3 Pour the softened cooled gelatin into the juice, making it up to 425 ml/3/4 pt with water.
4 Put the melon dice or balls into tall glasses and pour over the orange jelly. Refrigerate for a few hours until set.

Note: This recipe needs no sugar if the melon is ripe and the oranges are sweet.

FRUIT KEBABS Parev

A selection of fresh fruit which can be prepared in advance; do not use apples, pears or bananas as they discolour. (You will need some long wooden skewers.)

pineapple, melon, grapes, strawberries, clementines

To serve: Sponge cake or Pesach biscuits

1 Peel and prepare all the fruit. Cut pineapple and melons into large chunks, divide clementines into segments and wash grapes or strawberries.
2 Arrange the fruit in piles and then start to thread them on to long wooden skewers, alternating different coloured fruits.
3 Cover with clingfilm and refrigerate until serving.

EXOTIC FRUIT WITH BERRY COULIS Parev

kiwis, mangos, watermelon, sharon fruit, lychees, pawpaw
for the coulis: 250 g/8 oz raspberries or blackberries
1 heaped tbsp sugar

1 Peel the fruit and cut it into decorative slices.
2 Heat the berries with the sugar very gently (1 minute on HIGH in a microwave) or with a few spoonfuls of water in a small saucepan. When the juices start to run and the sugar is dissolved remove from the heat and press the berries through a sieve to remove the pips. Leave to cool.
3 Arrange the sliced fruits on large plates and pour some of the coulis in the centre.

STRAWBERRY AND BANANA 'CREME' BRULEE Milk

450 g pot low fat natural yogurt
2-4 tbsp sugar
17 5g/6 oz fresh strawberries, sliced
1 ripe banana, sliced

1 Unless you can buy thick set yogurt you need to drain it first. Line a large sieve with muslin or a sterilized handkerchief and set it over a bowl. Pour in the yogurt and leave it to drip, in the refrigerator, for at least one hour, preferably 3 - 4. You will then find that 2-4 fl oz (50-100 ml) liquid has dripped out. Pour this away and spoon the thick yogurt into the bowl. Stir in a little sugar to taste.
2 Arrange the sliced strawberries and banana in the base of four small ramekins and cover with the yogurt.
3 Put 2 tablespoons of sugar with 2 teaspoons of water in a very small pan and heat slowly until the sugar dissolves. Turn up the heat and boil until it starts to caramel. Immediately the colour changes from golden to dark brown, drizzle spoonfuls of the caramel over the four pots. The caramel will set immediately.

Note: You need to start early to make this variation on the traditional creme brulee. The amount of sugar you use depends on the natural sweetness of the strawberries and your particular taste, but remember that the caramel topping should contrast with the faint tartness of the yogurt and fruit and the finished dessert tastes quite different from the egg, cream and sugar combination of the real creme brulee.

CHOCOLATE ROULADE

Milk

(For this dessert you need a 9 inch square microwave dish)

4 eggs
75 g/3 oz vanilla sugar
115 g/4 oz good dark chocolate
2 tbsp sifted icing sugar
300 ml/1/2 pt fresh cream, whipped, or vanilla custard (see sauces)

1. Line the dish with greaseproof paper.
2. Break up the chocolate and cook in a bowl on MEDIUM with 3 tbsp water for about 2 minutes. Stir well until it is completely melted and leave to cool in the bowl.
3. Whisk the egg yolks with the sugar until light and fluffy. In a separate bowl whisk the whites until they are stiff.
4. Stir the cooled chocolate into the egg yolk mixture and then gently fold in the whites, distributing them evenly and avoiding any lumps. (Do not work the mixture too much.)
5. Spoon the mixture into the prepared dish and cook on HIGH for about 6-7 minutes until just set. It will rise and then fall and finally come away from the sides. Leave to cool for 5 minutes.
6. Sprinkle a fresh sheet of greaseproof paper with sifted icing sugar. Carefully turn over the cake, peel off the lining paper and then spread the cold whipped cream or custard over the cake. Lift the paper and roll the cake over once and then again on to a flat dish. Tuck in the edges and any cream which is oozing out. Leave to get cold but don't refrigerate or it will go hard.
7. Just before serving sprinkle over a little extra icing sugar.

LITTLE CHOCOLATE POTS

Milk

350 g/12 oz dark chocolate
2 tbsp unsalted butter
300 ml/1/2 pt milk
2 large eggs
3 tbsp chocolate or
coffee liqueur

To serve: Single cream (optional)

1. Melt the chocolate and butter together in a bowl on HIGH for about 1-2 minutes, stirring once and removing when the chocolate is soft.
2. Stir it vigorously and then pour it into a liquidizer with the milk and process for about 30 seconds. Add the eggs and continue until the mixture is smooth. Stir in the liqueur.
3. Pour the mixture into small individual pots and chill in the refrigerator for a few hours. Serve with a jug of single cream.

APPLES WITH ORANGE SAUCE

Parev

4 coxes apples (or other eating apples, but not Bramleys)

To serve: Orange sauce (see sauces) fresh grapes or clementines

1. Peel the apples and cut them into quarters. Remove the core and cut again to make 8 sections out of each one. Arrange all the apple pieces round the outside of two large plates, leaving the centre uncovered.
2. Cover and cook on HIGH for 2 minutes for each plate. Leave to cool.
3. Make the orange sauce and spoon some into the centre of individual plates. Arrange the apple slices in a circle round the sauce and decorate with a few seedless grapes or clementine segments.

CREME CARAMEL

Milk

4 tbsp sugar
2 eggs
300 ml/1/2 pt milk

1. Have ready four small ramekin dishes (glass or china, but not plastic).
2. Heat the milk on HIGH in a jug for 1 minute.
3. Put 2 heaped tablespoons of sugar into a very small pan with one tablespoon of water and heat gently until the sugar has dissolved. Turn up the heat and cook, without stirring, until the sugar begins to turn brown. Immediately pour the caramel into the base of the four pots, swirling it round the bottom.
4. Whisk the eggs with the remaining sugar and stir in the hot milk. Strain this into the ramekins, filling each one two-thirds full.
5. Arrange the ramekins around the edge of the turntable and microwave on LOW/MEDIUM for about 7 minutes. The mixture should cook gently but should not be allowed to boil, so watch it carefully after about four minutes and turn the power down if the mixture is bubbling.
6. Leave to stand until cool and then refrigerate for a few hours. Pass a knife round the edges of each ramekin and put a saucer over the top. Turn them over and press down, shaking the ramekin to release the creme caramel. The sauce will be quite liquid and will surround the set custard.

Note: This amount makes 4 small pots. To increase the quantities, double the ingredients and allow 10-12 minutes cooking time.

POACHED PEARS IN LEMON SYRUP

Parev

50 g/2 oz sugar
175 ml/6 fl oz water
juice of 1 lemon (about 2 tbsp)
4 large conference pears

1. Put the sugar and water in a bowl and cook on HIGH for 3 minutes. Add the lemon juice and continue boiling on HIGH for a further 3 minutes.
2. While the syrup is cooking peel the pears. Cut them in halves and remove the cores.
3. Arrange the pears in a single layer in a shallow dish, pour over the syrup, cover and cook on HIGH for about 4 minutes. (It may take slightly less or more time depending on how ripe the pears are. They should be just tender.) Carefully remove the cover to see if the pears are done (there will be a lot of steam) and leave them to cool. Serve in a decorative glass dish.

ORANGE SAUCE

Parev

2 eggs
2 tbsp sugar
juice and rind of 2 oranges
1 tbsp potato flour

1. With a zester remove a few orange shreds from the skin for decoration. Grate a little more of the rind to add to the custard.
2. Mix the eggs with the sugar, potato flour and orange juice and about a tablespoon of rind.
3. Heat the mixture on MEDIUM for about 2 minutes, stirring several times until it begins to thicken. Leave to cool.
4. Serve with cooked apples or pears and garnish with some of the orange shreds.

APRICOT PUREE

Parev

6-8 large fresh apricots
1 tsp sugar
1 tsp lemon juice

1. Halve the apricots and remove the stones. Sprinkle over the sugar and cook them in a small container, covered, on HIGH for about 2 minutes.
2. Stir in the lemon juice and pass the fruit through a strainer. Taste for sweetness, adding more sugar if you are using the puree as a dessert or more lemon juice if you are serving it with roast or grilled duck.

Note: The sauce can be made with dried apricots (in which case the sugar should be omitted). Cover with boiling water and microwave on HIGH for 1 minute. Leave to stand for about half an hour to plump up and abosrb some of the water and then cook as above until they are soft.

VANILLA CUSTARD SAUCE

Milk

2 tsp potato flour
2 tbsp vanilla sugar
2 small eggs or 3 egg yolks
300 ml/1/2 pt milk

1. Mix the potato flour in a bowl with the sugar. (If you have a vanilla pod you can scrape out the grains and add these too as it will give the sauce a much richer flavour.)
2. Stir in the eggs and add the milk.
3. Microwave on MEDIUM for 2-3 minutes, opening the door and stirring frequently. When the sauce is thick, stir again and immediately stand the bowl in cold water. Leave to cool.
4. For a pouring sauce, you may need to add a little extra milk. Otherwise spoon out the custard and serve it with cooked apples, pears, rhubarb or apricots.

TOMATO SAUCE

Parev. Vegetarian

350 g/12 oz very ripe tomatoes
1 tbsp olive oil
1 onion, finely chopped
1/2 tsp sugar
salt, pepper
2 tsp tomato puree (optional)
few leaves fresh basil, chopped

1 Immerse the tomatoes in boiling water for a few seconds, until the skins peel off easily. Chop the tomatoes roughly.
2 Heat the olive oil in a dish on HIGH for about 50 seconds and stir in the onion. Cook for 3 minutes, stirring once, until the onion has softened.
3 Add the chopped tomatoes with their juice, the sugar, salt and pepper and cook for another 3 minutes.
4 Leave to cool slightly, then sieve the sauce into a bowl. Test the seasoning and add the tomato puree if the taste is not strong enough (this depends on the natural flavour of the tomatoes). Stir in a little chopped basil and reserve the rest to sprinkle over the top.

LEMON SAUCE

Meat or Parev. Vegetarian

2 egg yolks
juice of 1/2 lemon
75 ml/3 fl oz light vegetable or chicken stock, warmed

1 Mix the egg yolks with the lemon juice in a jug and stir in the warm stock. Cook on MEDIUM for 1 minute. Stir and cook for another minute, stopping once or twice to stir again to make sure the sauce does not curdle. It will thicken slightly as it heats.
2 Leave the sauce to stand for a few minutes and serve warm with vegetables, fish or chicken.

WINE AND CHEESE SAUCE

Milk. Vegetarian

4 tsp potato flour
1 small egg
300 ml/1/2pt warm milk
salt, pepper
100 g/4 oz grated hard cheese
3-4 tbsp white wine

1 In a bowl or jug, mix the potato flour with the egg, a little salt, pepper and milk and stir well.
2 Heat the mixture on HIGH for 1 minute, stirring twice. When it starts to thicken add 25 g/1 oz cheese and the wine, and continue cooking on MEDIUM for half a minute. Stir in the remaining cheese, taste for seasoning and serve immediately.

Note: Reheating the sauce once the cheese has been added may make it separate.

NOTES FOR NEXT YEAR